SHARK FILES

DOSSIERS SUR LES REQUINS

GREAT WHITE SHARKS
LES GRANDS REQUINS BLANCS

Written by/Autere: Julie K. Lundgren

A Crabtree Seedlings Book

Un livre de la collection
Les jeunes plantes de Crabtree

TABLE OF CONTENTS
TABLE DES MATIÈRES

Crabtree Publishing
crabtreebooks.com

School-to-Home Support for Caregivers and Teachers

This book helps children grow by letting them practice reading. Here are a few guiding questions to help the reader with building his or her comprehension skills. Possible answers appear here in red.

Before Reading:

- What do I think this book is about?
  - *I think this book is about great white sharks.*
  - *I think this book will tell me what they eat.*
- What do I want to learn about this topic?
  - *I want to learn where great white sharks live.*
  - *I want to learn how many teeth they have.*

During Reading:

- I wonder why...
  - *I wonder what tools are used to study great white sharks.*
  - *I wonder why people kill sharks for their teeth.*
- What have I learned so far?
  - *I have learned that each shark's fin is unique like fingerprints.*
  - *I have learned that they swim in both deep and shallow waters.*

After Reading:

- What details did I learn about this topic?
  - *I have learned that great white sharks are the deadliest hunters in the sea.*
  - *I have learned that they catch and eat rays, sea turtles, and California sea lions.*
- Read the book again and look for the vocabulary words.
  - *I see the word lurk on page 6 and the word dorsal on page 16. The other glossary words are on pages 22 and 23.*

Soutien de l'école à la maison pour les parents, les gardiens et les enseignants

Ce livre aide les enfants à se développer grâce à la pratique de la lecture. Voici quelques exemples de questions pour aider le lecteur ou la lectrice à développer ses capacités de compréhension. Les suggestions de réponses sont indiquées en rouge.

Avant la lecture

- De quoi ce livre parle-t-il?
  - *Je pense que ce livre parle des grands requins blancs.*
  - *Je pense que ce livre me dira ce qu'ils mangent.*
- Qu'est-ce que je veux apprendre sur ce sujet?
  - *Je veux savoir où vivent les grands requins blancs.*
  - *Je veux savoir combien de dents ils ont.*

Pendant la lecture

- Je me demande pourquoi...
  - *Je me demande quels outils sont utilisés pour étudier les grands requins blancs.*
  - *Je me demande pourquoi les gens tuent les requins pour leurs dents.*
- Qu'est-ce que j'ai appris jusqu'à présent?
  - *J'ai appris que chaque nageoire du requin est unique, comme les empreintes digitales.*
  - *J'ai appris qu'ils nagent autant dans les eaux profondes que peu profondes.*

Après la lecture

- Nomme quelques détails que tu as retenus.
  - *J'ai appris que les grands requins blancs sont les chasseurs les plus meurtriers de la mer.*
  - *J'ai appris qu'ils attrapent et mangent des raies, des tortues de mer et des otaries de Californie.*
- Lis le livre à nouveau et cherche les mots de vocabulaire.
  - *Je vois le mot* ***rôdent*** *à la page 6 et le mot* ***dorsale*** *à la page 16. Les autres mots du glossaire se trouvent aux pages 22 et 23.*

GREAT WHITE SHARKS

Which fish is the deadliest hunter in the sea?

LE GRAND REQUIN BLANC

Quel poisson est le chasseur le plus meurtrier de la mer?

Great white sharks! They catch big **prey**.

Le grand requin blanc! Il attrape de grosses **proies**.

ray
raie

sea turtle
tortue de mer

California sea lion
otarie de Californie

FROM THE FILES

Rays, sea turtles, and California sea lions are prey for great whites.

INFO AU DOSSIER

Les raies, les tortues de mer et les otaries de Californie sont des proies pour les grands blancs.

Great whites **lurk** below, then speed to their prey above.

Les grands blancs **rôdent** sous leur proie, puis montent rapidement pour les attraper.

They can feel movement from **distant** animals.

Ils peuvent sentir les mouvements des animaux **lointains**.

FROM THE FILES

Great whites can see and hear well.

INFO AU DOSSIER

Les grands blancs peuvent très bien voir et entendre.

Sharp **teeth** slice food. Gulp!

Leurs **dents** acérées tranchent la nourriture. Gloup!

They swim in both deep and **shallow** waters.

Ils nagent autant dans les eaux profondes que **peu profondes**.

Tools help us study sharks.

Des outils nous aident à étudier les requins.

Each shark has a **dorsal** fin that is not like any other shark's.

Chaque requin a une nageoire **dorsale** qui ne ressemble à aucune autre.

FROM THE FILES

We know each shark by its fin, like a fingerprint!

INFO AU DOSSIER

Nous connaissons chaque requin par sa nageoire, comme une empreinte digitale.

People kill sharks for their jaws, teeth, and fins.

Les gens tuent les requins pour prendre leurs mâchoires, leurs dents et leurs nageoires.

There is much more to learn about great white sharks.

Il y a beaucoup plus à apprendre au sujet des grands requins blancs.

GLOSSARY/GLOSSAIRE

distant (DISS-tehnt): Distant animals or objects are far away.
lointains (lo-in-tin) : Les animaux ou objets lointains sont à grande distance.

dorsal (DOR-suhl): A dorsal fin is the fin on top of a shark's back.
dorsale (dor-sal) : Une nageoire dorsale est celle qui se trouve sur le dos d'un requin.

lurk (LERK): To lurk is to hide in sneaky silence.
rôdent (reaud) : Rôder signifie se cacher sournoisement en silence.

prey (PRAY): Prey is any animal hunted and eaten by another animal.
proie (proa) : Une proie est tout animal chassé et mangé par un autre animal.

shallow (SHAL-oh): Shallow water is not deep and is often near land.
peu profonde (peu pro-fon-de): L'eau peu profonde est souvent située près des terres.

teeth (TEETH): Teeth are white, bony parts inside a mouth that are used for biting and chewing.
dents (dan) : Les dents sont des organes de la bouche, blancs et osseux, qui sont utilisés pour mordre et mâcher.

Index

Index

About the Author/À propos de l'auteure

Julie K. Lundgren

Julie K. Lundgren grew up near Lake Superior where she reveled in mucking about in the woods, picking berries, and expanding her rock collection. Her interests led her to a degree in biology. She lives in Minnesota with her family.

Julie K. Lundgren a grandi près du lac Supérieur, où elle s'amusait dans les bois, cueillait des baies et enrichissait sa collection de pierres. Ses intérêts l'ont conduite à un diplôme en biologie. Elle vit au Minnesota avec sa famille.

Websites/Sites Web

Les sites Web sont en anglais seulement.

www.montereybayaquarium.org/animals/animals-a-to-z/white-shark
www.natgeokids.com/uk/discover/animals/sea-life/great-white-sharks

---

Crabtree Publishing

crabtreebooks.com 800-387-7650

Hardcover: 978-1-0398-6995-0
Paperback: 978-1-0398-6983-7
Ebook (pdf): 978-1-0398-7007-9
Epub: 978-1-0398-7019-2

Printed in Canada/

Library and Archives Canada Cataloguing in Publication
Available at the Library and Archives Canada

Library of Congress Cataloging-in-Publication Data
Available at the Library of Congress

Published in Canada
Publié au Canada
Crabtree Publishing
616 Welland Ave.
St. Catharines, Ontario
L2M 5V6

Published in the United States
Publié aux États-Unis
Crabtree Publishing
347 Fifth Ave
Suite 1402-145
New York, NY 10016

Photographs/Photographies:
Shark illustration on cover logo © BATKA/Shutterstock; white shark illustration for "FROM THE FILES" © Dashikka/Shutterstock; Cover photo © Sergey Uryadnikov/Shutterstock; Page 3 © RamonCarretero/istock; page 4 (ray and sea turtle) © richcarey, (sea lion) © GlobalP/istock; page 5 © USO/istock; page 7 © Sergey Uryadnikov/Shutterstock; page 9 © Ramon Carretero/Shutterstock; page 11 © Martin Prochazkacz/Shutterstock; page 12 © Willyam Bradberry/Shutterstock; page 13 © Brent Barnes | Dreamstime.com; page 15 (top) © Stefan Pircher/Shutterstock, (bottom) © OCEARCH/R. Snow; page 17 © Sergey Uryadnikov/Shutterstock; page 18 © Alessandro De Maddalena/Shutterstock; page 19 © Andrey Simonenko | Dreamstime.com; page 21 © USO/istock; page 22 (top photo) © Aerial-motion/Shutterstock

Author/Auteure : Julie K. Lundgren
Designed by/Conception : Jennifer Dydyk
Edited by/Révision : Kelli Hicks
Proofreader/Correctrice : Melissa Boyce
Translation/Traduction : Annie Evearts